INTRODUCTION

In the years that immediately followed the end of the Second World War, there were hopes that the alliance that had been forged between the western allies and the Soviet Union for the purpose of defeating Nazi Germany might continue to develop and strengthen. Such hopes, however, were soon shown to be illusory as the aggressive expansionist policies of Stalinist Russia became apparent through actions such as the blockade of Berlin in 1948–49 and the subjugation one after the other, of countries in eastern Europe through the imposition of communist regimes.

The formation of the North Atlantic Treaty Organization (NATO) in 1949 proved effective in halting further Soviet expansion westward, but in the following year the outbreak of war in Korea showed that the USSR was intent on throwing its weight into proxy wars elsewhere on the planet, and there was no guarantee that the Russians would not one day turn against their former wartime allies. For the NATO planners, it was a nightmare scenario made worse by a lack of intelligence on the Soviet Union's true military capability.

For the first five years of the post-war period, the strength of Soviet military power in Eastern Europe was greatly overestimated. Soviet armoured forces, it was estimated in 1949–50, could field 35,000 tanks, of which 20,000 were classed as first-line tanks (mainly T-54s and T-10s) and 20,000 as second-line (mainly T-34s and IS-3s). In other words, the conventional balance seemed to be heavily weighted in favour of the Soviet Union, especially in terms of tank strength. Although the numbers of operationally-ready Soviet tanks were greatly exaggerated, however, they were still sufficient to overwhelm NATO forces in the event of a massed attack into western Germany, for NATO's armoured forces were still undergoing a period of regeneration. They were, for the most part,

still equipped with the Sherman, and M47 Patton tanks, which the allies well in the closing the Second World War, but replacements were slow to arrive in the series of American Patton Tanks, the M48, would not be available for initial deployment until at least 1952, while the French, making herculean efforts to re-establish their own military production, would not have an indigenous MBT until the mid-1960s.

The British, with their Centurion MBT, were much better placed to counter the potential Soviet armoured threat. The armoured regiments of the British Army of the Rhine (BAOR) had begun to receive the Centurion in 1946, and the tank was also issued to other NATO armies in the mid-1950s with the help of American funding, but it had already become clear that the Centurion, effective though it was, would need to be supplanted within the next decade by a Main Battle Tank armed with a new 120mm main gun.

Development of the new MBT was initiated in 1951. It would be called the Chieftain.

Soviet tanks in Berlin. The Russians maintained huge quantities of armour in eastern Germany after the war ended, making the deployment of new Allied Main Battle Tanks imperative.

The 6th Armoured Division, 29th March 1945. The M4A3(76) W HVSS has field workshop-applied additional armour cut from destroyed tanks.

Development & Design

The basic requirement for the new MBT, initially known as the Medium Gun Tank Mk 2 and later allocated the designation FV4201, was that it was to be at least as capable as the Centurion, with emphasis on battlefield agility at the expense of maximum speed. Put simply, the intention was to produce a tank combining the firepower of a 120mm gun with the reliability and versatility of the Centurion. Firepower was a key component; the tank was expected to engage the enemy at long range from defensive positions, and to be proof against medium artillery. It was to have a firing rate of ten rounds per minute in the first minute and six rounds per minute in the following four. Overall weight of the tank was not to exceed forty-five tons, which in itself created a problem if a heavy large-calibre main gun were to be installed.

The choice of armament was a matter that demanded a great deal of investigation by the design leaders, Vickers, the weapons experts at the Royal Armament Research and Development Establishment (RARDE) at Fort Halstead in Kent and the Fighting Vehicles Research and Development Establishment (FVRDE) at Chertsey in Surrey. Several proposals were considered and rejected in turn, including one for a liquid propellant tank gun under investigation by the US Army in the 1950s.

A much more promising concept was the bagged charge, in which the projectile was inserted into the breech followed by the explosive propellant in a bag. This arrangement had been used in naval gunnery for many years, using cordite, a mixture of nitro-glycerine and gun cotton dissolved in acetone, and stabilized by adding a small amount of Vaseline. The charge was contained in a bag of pure silk. Behind the cordite charge a small quantity

of gunpowder in a tube was placed to assist ignition, as cordite did not catch fire readily. The gunpowder was electrically ignited by means of a fine wire inserted in the tube, which glowed white-hot when the firing sequence was initiated.

The bagged charge option was attractive for a number of reasons, not the least of which was that it occupied less stowage space than single-piece ammunition, permitting more rounds to be carried. It was also easier for the loader to handle, and trials showed that the use of two-piece ammunition did not reduce the required firing rate. The plan was to stow the bagged charges in water jackets below the turret ring, a system whereby the charges would be doused by a mixture of water and glycol should they be penetrated by hot shell or armour fragments. The armour piercing ammunition, which had no explosive content, could then be stored in the interior of the turret and in external stowage bins.

In 1957 RARDE at Fort Halstead designed a new 120mm rifled tank gun, the L11, for use in the Chieftain tank. The gun was of conventional design with a semi-automatic breech mechanism, which opened the breech after firing and made it ready for reloading. A vent tube holder at the rear of the breech ring facilitated electric firing of the bagged charge. The barrel was of monobloc construction, featuring a fume extractor and a thermal sleeve. The main production model was the L11A5, which introduced an integral muzzle reference system, an electronic device designed to measure the current value of a tank barrel bend (the slight 'droop' caused by gravity and temperature differences) and transmit it into the tank's fire control system to cancel out firing errors by correcting the relevant aiming angles. The system consisted of a reflector installed at the gun muzzle end of the barrel and a measuring unit installed on the barrel near the gun mantlet. The L11 was the first tank gun of its type and calibre to be fitted with this system, which later became a feature of all modern MBT guns.

One major innovation of the FV4201 design was that the driver was seated in a semi-recumbent position when his hatch was closed down, which reduced the profile of the forward glacis plate and enabled it to be heavily sloped, with a thickness of

A mockup of the FV4201 Chieftain design, which was intended to incorporate all the best qualities of the Centurion with the firepower of a 120mm main gun. (Wikimedia Commons)

15.3in (388mm). Another, which turned out to be unfortunate, was the choice of engine. Originally, the intention had been to use a new Rolls-Royce V-8 diesel engine as the powerplant, but in 1957, the NATO Standardization Committee decreed that all fighting vehicles operated by the Alliance were to be powered by multi-fuel engines – in other words, engines that were capable of running on whatever fuel was available, ranging from diesel through petrol and paraffin to domestic heating oil. It seemed a sensible arrangement, as it would enable fighting vehicles to refuel just about anywhere, but it was to produce serious shortcomings that were not envisaged at the time.

The new powerplant-developed by British Leyland with some input from Rolls-Royce – was the L60, a nineteen-litre vertical six-cylinder opposed-piston two-stroke diesel engine based on a wartime German design, the Junkers Jumo 205, which had two crankshafts geared together and which powered such aircraft types as the massive Blohm und Voss Bv 222 flying boat. Engines of similar design had also been produced by Napier and Tilling-Stevens. The chosen configuration, apart from being well suited to multi-fuel use, also had the advantages of being of simple design with a low parts count, low bearing loads, and possessing good cold-starting characteristics, although an unforeseen complication was that it experienced substantial thermal stress problems. Both Tilling-Stevens and Leyland produced single-cylinder prototype engines for the tank engine project and by 1959 the resulting complete engine design had become the Leyland 60, or L60, with the first engine running that same year. The early BL Engine delivered around 450bhp (340kW) to the sprocket, which meant that top road speed was limited to around 25mph (40km/h), and cross-country performance was reduced. The latter was further hampered by the Horstmann coil spring suspension, which made for an uncomfortable ride.

The particular feature of this engine was that, for good combustion, it needed the ignition delay to be reduced, thus requiring the internal temperature inside the cylinder after compression to be higher than usual. Engine research started in 1952 and led, in 1956, to the adoption of a family of 6-cylinder opposed-piston engines, like the two-stroke truck diesel, the Rootes TS-3. The latter inspired the LM L60, but with a different mechanical layout. Whereas in the TS-3 pistons were connected by rocker levers to a single crankshaft, the L60 took the path of the 1930s Junkers Jumo diesel, with two crankshafts geared together. But this formula experienced substantial thermal stress problems.

The technical solution adopted for the diesel proved unfit for multifuel use and prevented it from reaching the planned output of 700hp without consequences

for the piston and cylinder lining. These issues and the overall weight resulted in a catastrophic 90% breakdown rate in exercises for the Mark I series, never really completely solved, but the output was raised in 1967. Later, additional armour and equipment added their own weight to the problem. In 1974, the newly introduced Belzona variant (named for the type of epoxy resin coating introduced to protect liner seals) gave 850hp, which was a great improvement compared to the original BL with 450bhp. The final speed was around 48km/h (30mph) on road, still below the performance of the new Challenger, and dictated a specific tactical use when operating in combination with the latter. With years of tactical exercises and well-understood limitations, the Chieftain proved a formidable asset in the British Army arsenal.

In August 1958 the General Staff issued a detailed requirement – not yet a Specification – for the design of FV4201, together with authorization for the construction of a wooden mock-up. With the design of the latter generally accepted, Leyland received an order to proceed with the construction of six prototypes (P1 to P6). Early trials with these vehicles revealed a number of snags, the most serious of which involved engine vibration and faults with the cooling system. To rectify these the rear hull had to be redesigned, increasing the design weight from forty-five to nearly

The Leyland L60 engine pack, with one of the radiators in the raised position, on display at the Bovington Tank Museum. The L60 was a nineteen-litre vertical six-cylinder opposed-piston two-stroke diesel engine based on a wartime German design, the Junkers Jumo 205. (Wikimedia Commons)

The tanks that formed the backbone of the British Army of the Rhine in the 1960s: the heavy Conqueror, the Centurion (a Mk 7 illustrated) and the Chieftain. (Wikipedia Commons)

At one point, consideration was given to fitting the Chieftain with a liquid propellant main gun. This illustration shows an experimental US vehicle armed with a 155 liquid propellant weapon. (Source unknown)

fifty tons and requiring the suspension to be redesigned to cope with the extra load. Track pads had to be fitted to protect roads from damage in the BAOR's West German exercise areas, and the ground clearance was increased.

Prototype P1 was delivered to the FVRDE in January 1960, followed by P2 in April. As both were intended purely for running trials, they were not fitted with turrets. It was at this point that problems with the multi-fuel engine concept became apparent. The rather rosy view that the engine could be switched from one fuel type to another at the flick of a switch turned out to be illusion, the trials revealing that it would take at least eight hours to make the change. The multi-fuel concept was soon abandoned by other tank-producing NATO countries, which adopted standard diesel engines; only the British and French pursued the idea, and although in practice the L60 engine used only diesel fuel, the powerplant itself continued to be troublesome.

Meanwhile, six more FV4201 prototypes (W1 to W6) had been built, and in May 1961 W3 went to the gunnery ranges at Kirkudbright in Scotland for firing trials with the 120mm L11 gun, testing of the gun control equipment having been completed in the previous year. The original Fire Control System (FCS) was the Marconi FV/GCE Mk 4. A 0.50in (12.7mm) ranging gun was mounted above the main gun (with 300 rounds available). This fired ranging shots out to a maximum of 2,600 yards (2,400m), at which point the tracer in the ranging rounds burned out although the high explosive tip still created a visible 'splash' on impact. The tank commander had a rotating cupola with nine vision blocks giving all-round view, plus the 7.62mm machine gun and an infrared (IR) capable projector coaxial with the weapon. The aiming systems were provided for both the gunner and the tank commander; they had 1x or 10x selectable magnification power (increasing to 15x in the Mk 5 and beyond), and they were interchangeable with IR vision systems for night operations (3x magnification power). The commander could rotate his cupola to bring his sight onto a target and then engage the mechanism that brought the turret round on to the correct bearing so that the gunner could complete the aiming. The firing trials were a complete success, although a number of recommendations were made, one of which was to replace the 0.50in ranging gun with a co-axial 7.62mm Browning machine gun.

In 1962, selected tank crews from the 1st and 5th Royal Tank Regiments, then armed with Centurions and based on Hohne and Fallingbostel in the BAOR, were sent to the UK for familiarization with the new tank,

Several aspects of the Chieftain were tested in the FV4202, seen here. It was known as the 40-ton Centurion, and this is one of only three units built. (Tank Museum)

A Chieftain of 1 RTR in Germany, with a Westland Lynx helicopter of the Army Air Corps hovering overhead. (MoD)

which by this time was officially known as the Chieftain. At the end of the year, prototypes W1 and W3, which incorporated all the modifications and recommendations resulting from earlier trials, were shipped to the BAOR for field testing and comparison with the Centurion Mk 7. It soon became apparent that there was still work to be done before the tank could be accepted for service. For one thing, the suspension needed to be modified to provide extra ground clearance, and the electro-mechanical equipment used for ramming the projectile into the breech was found to be unreliable. In practice, it proved more effective for the bagged charge to be used as the rammer, a procedure that was adopted in production vehicles.

Despite the fact that further modifications were necessary, the Chieftain was accepted for production on 1 May 1963, and an order was placed for 40 Chieftain Mk 1 tanks, which were issued to 1 and 5 RTR in 1965–66 and used for training. Production was shared between the Royal Ordnance Factory at Leeds (26 units) and Vickers-Armstrong (14 units). The Mk 1s were soon followed by the first viable production model, the Mk 2, the first six being issued to the 11th Hussars at Hohne, near Hannover, in November 1966.

Chieftains on manoeuvres with the BAOR. By the time all its modifications had been completed, the Chieftain was the best Main Battle Tank in service with NATO's armoured divisions. (MoD)

The Chieftain in Detail

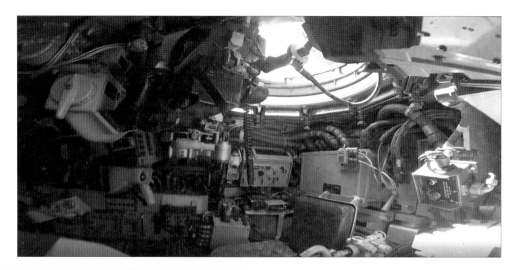

Interior of the Chieftain's turret, looking up towards the commander's cupola. (Source unknown)

Exterior of the Chieftain's turret, with the commander's access hatch open. (Source unknown)

The driving compartment

Access to the driver's compartment was by way of a hatch located in the upper glacis plate. The driver, in his reclined seat, had a view of the outside world when the tank was closed down via an AFV No 36 Mk 1 wide-angle periscope sight, which could be exchanged for an infra-red sight for night driving. The sight was fitted with both washer and wiper systems to enable the driver to clean it when the vehicle was closed down. The driver steered by means of two conventional levers; also conventional were his three foot pedals, the accelerator pedal on the right and the footbrake in the centre. On the left was an electro-mechanical foot pedal, which could be flicked up or pressed down by the driver's toe to change gear as required.

The fighting compartment

The fighting compartment housed the other three crew members in a turret extending the full width of the hull, the turret being seated on a ball race to allow a full 360-degree rotation. Unlike earlier main battle tanks, there was no large armoured gun mantlet, which had been replaced by a narrow aperture for the 120mm main gun. The front part of the turret was of a single casting, the rest consisting of rolled and welded armour plate. The commander and gunner were seated to the right of the main armament and the gunner to its left. The commander's position was elevated and he was seated under a cupola that could also be traversed through 360 degrees to provide all-round vision through nine observation periscopes and one sighting periscope. A spotlight was mounted on the exterior of the cupola, as was a 7.62mm machine gun. The commander could rotate his cupola to bring his sight onto a target and then engage a mechanism that brought the turret round on to the correct bearing so that the gunner could complete the aiming process.

The engine compartment

The engine compartment housed the engine, auxiliary generating engine and transmission, the whole ensemble being called the power pack. A platform on top of this had access covers to the coolant and hydraulic oil compartments, while the main engine deck panels, on either side of the engine, lifted outwards to

The sharp end: a closeup of the Chieftain's 120mm main gun. The mounting atop the muzzle is a component of the muzzle reference system, an electronic device intended to measure the current value of a tank barrel bend in order to take it into account when firing the gun and therefore improve the accuracy of firing. (Wikimedia Commons)

reveal two radiators which could be lifted outwards to give access to the L60 engine, auxiliary generator and air cleaners. The transmission was situated at the rear of the compartment under its own deck panels. The TN12 transmission, originally designed by Self-Changing Gears Ltd, was installed in all production Chieftains. The whole power pack could be lifted out as a single unit for major servicing. Although the engine underwent numerous modifications to increase its efficiency, the basic layout remained unchanged from the Chieftain Mk 1 to the Mk 11. All incorporated epicyclic geartrains in the change speed section to give six forward and two reverse speeds. Vehicle steering was achieved by a fully regenerative Merritt-Brown triple-differential system which maintained power during turns and provided an axis steer capability for high manoeuvrability.

By eliminating unnecessary clutches, all TN12 units featured high mechanical efficiency, giving higher sprocket power for a given gross engine power. In addition, a corresponding reduction of burden on, and therefore size of, cooling group could often be achieved. Designs of intermediate versions between TN12 and TN12-1000 existed for both new vehicles and replacement engines in existing TN12 installations in Chieftain MBTs.

The hull

The Chieftain's hull was of welded steel armour plate, with the floor plate shaped into a V-type section to give protection against mines. As an additional measure, the hull sides were sloped outwards to divert mine blast.

The redesign of the rear hull, found to be necessary during early trials, and other additions such as track pads, raised the design weight to close on fifty tons. Frontal armour thickness was 388mm (15.3in)

and the sides 195mm (1.37in). From the Chieftain Mk 10, the design incorporated Stillbrew armour (named after Colonel Still and John Brewer of the Military Vehicles and Engineering Establishment), which provided extra protection against the 125mm projectiles used by Russian T-62 and T-72 tanks. After highly successful firing and mobility trials in 1984 and 1985, Royal Ordnance Leeds began the manufacture of an applique armour package, which was fitted over the frontal aspect of the turret and around the driver's position to give additional protection to the turret ring. In 1986 BAOR Chieftains were upgraded with Stillbrew armour during routine overhaul at 23 REME Base Workshops at Wetter, West Germany.

CHIEFTAIN VARIANTS

FV4201 Prototypes

P1 to P6 delivered between January 1960 and November 1962, followed by W1 to W6 between March 1961 and April 1962. Two further vehicles, G1 and G2 (in effect pre-production vehicles) were delivered in January and November 1962.

Stillbrew turret armour seen on a Chieftain Mk 11 MBT. In the 1990s Chobham armour plating was also fitted to Chieftain AVREs for additional protection. (Via Del Lewis)

Chieftain Mk 1

Production of the Chieftain Mk 1 began in May 1963, the work being shared between the Royal Ordnance Factory at Barnbow, Leeds, and Vickers-Armstrong at Elswick, Newcastle upon Tyne. Forty units were produced, but with an engine producing only 585bhp and ongoing problems with the L60 engine and TN12 gearbox they were used for training purposes, experiencing a ninety percent unserviceability rate. The Chieftain Mk 1 was identified by split hatches on the commander's cupola, similar to those on later marks of the Centurion. The basic Mk 1 was subject to a number of improvements during its service life, the Mk 1/1 having a modified exhaust system and engine air cleaner, while further improvements to the exhaust system, a new cupola, modified smoke dischargers, the addition of four headlights – two white and two infra-red – resulted in the Mk 1/2.

Built by Vickers, this Chieftain Mk 1 00EB12, with Stillbrew, shows it paces at the East of England Military Museum near Thetford, Suffolk.

The Chieftain Mk 2 was the first fully operational variant to serve with the British Army. Although it evolved into a superb tank, its early problems, especially with the engine, deterred many potential customers. (Norfolk Tank Museum)

Chieftain Mk 2

The Chieftain Mk 2, fitted with a much-improved 650bhp engine, was the first variant to be declared fully operational with the British Army. Improvements, which included a new turret with better protection and rear hull sealing for deep wading, were all made during manufacture. The first delivery was made by ROF Leeds on 18 April 1966, the first tanks replacing the Centurions of the 11th Hussars.

This Chieftain Mk 2, preserved in the Bovington Tank Museum, had the names 'Mr Bill' and then 'Boudicca' painted in its side stowage boxes. (Tank Museum)

The Chieftain Mk 2.

Chieftain Mk 3

This variant was basically a Mk 2 with stronger suspension units. It also featured an improved starting system for low temperature operation. Other refinements included improved ammunition stowage, strengthened trackguards and a revised commander's cupola with angled periscopes to reduce glare and a 7.62mm L37A1 general purpose machine gun. The basic Mk 3 gave rise to many sub-variants, modifications being made during the vehicle's service life. The last of these, the Mk 3/3, had a modified hull to accommodate the new 720bhp L60 engine.

Chieftain Mk 4

Two vehicles were built at ROF Leeds to an Israeli specification, but a planned production order was cancelled in 1969 and the vehicles (02SP95 and 02SP96) were shipped to the USA, where they carried out desert trials at the US Army's Yuma Proving Ground in Arizona from May to September 1971.

Chieftain Mk 5

Developed from the Mk 3 and incorporating all the improvements made to date, the Mk 5 was the definitive production version of the Chieftain. The first vehicle was delivered from ROF Leeds in March 1972.

Chieftain production progressed through the Mk 6 to the Mk 11, this being the final version issued to the British Army. All these marks incorporated modifications, some of a minor nature. Much thought was given to enhancing survivability, and the Mk 10 incorporated Stillbrew passive armour

The Chieftain Mk 2.

A Chieftain Mk 3 with Stillbrew seen in the collection of the Israeli Armoured Corps Museum at Latrun. (IDF)

One of two Chieftain Mk 4 tanks built at ROF Leeds to an Israeli specification in anticipation of an Israeli order, subsequently cancelled. After desert trials in the USA the vehicles were returned to the UK one of them being used to test the Hydrogas suspension system. (Tank Museum)

(named after Colonel Still and John Brewer of the Military Vehicles and Engineering Establishment), which provided extra protection against the 125mm projectiles used by Russian T-62 and T-72 tanks. Earlier marks of the Chieftain were brought up to Mk 5 standard through the so-called 'Totem Pole' conversion programme, which introduced progressive improvements to the fire control system and automotive package.

The Chieftain Mk 12/13 were proposed further upgrades, but were cancelled with the introduction of the Challenger I.

Chieftain Specification (Mk 5)

Armament: One 120mm (4.72in) L11A5 gun, two 7.62mm (0.3in) MGs, one 12.7mm (0.5in) MG

Armour: not available

Crew: 4

Dimensions: Length 7.518m (24ft 8in); Width 3.50m (11ft 6in); Height 2.895m (9ft 6in)

Weight: 55,000kg (54.13 tons)

Powerplant: Leyland L60 multi-fuel developing 559.2kW (750bhp) at 2100rpm

Speed: 48km/h (30mph)

Range: 400–500km (248.5–280 miles)

A Chieftain Mk 6 becomes the centre of attraction at a British Army display. (MoD)

The Chieftain Mk 11, seen here in Middle East camouflage, was the final gun tank variant to serve with the British Army. (Via Del Lewis)

All Chieftains were eventually fitted with a thermal sleeve, seen here. Its function was to provide a more consistent temperature to the gun barrel, preventing distortions due to thermal expansion caused by temperature differences around the barrel during firing. (IDF)

Chieftain Mk 5 Main Battle Tank with 120mm gun at the North Cornwall Tank Collection. (Hugh Llewelyn)

Chieftain Engineering Vehicles

It was intended to replace the Centurion AVRE (Assault Vehicle Royal Engineers) with two variants of the Chieftain, both based on the Mk 5. These were the Chieftain Armoured Engineering Vehicle (Gun), fitted with a demolition gun, and the Chieftain Armoured Engineering Vehicle (Winch), both of which were to be multi-role vehicles capable of performing various functions. In the event, the AEV (Gun) was cancelled on financial grounds, but development work proceeded on the Chieftain AEV (Winch), which evolved into the FV4203 Chieftain AVRE in the early 1970s. This was to have been fitted with a dozer blade and deployable bridge, as well as road-laying equipment, but following a policy change this version was also cancelled after only two prototypes had been built, the plan now being to retain the Centurion AVRE in front-line service. Meanwhile, work went ahead with an ARV (Armoured Recovery Vehicle) conversion of the Chieftain, fitted with winches capable of recovering any armoured vehicle then in service and a dozer blade that could be dug in and used as an anchor while the recovery operation was in progress. In total, 257 Chieftain ARVs were built by Vickers at Elswick, Newcastle upon Tyne, the first being delivered to the British Army in 1974. Two Chieftain ARVs manned by REME crews were assigned to each armoured squadron in the Royal Armoured Corps. A further version was the Chieftain Armoured Repair and Recovery Vehicle (CHARRV), mounting a hydraulic crane.

A bridgelayer variant of the Chieftain Mk 5, known as the AVLB (Armoured Vehicle Launched Bridge), was developed to replace the Centurion Mk 5 Bridgelayer, the first examples being delivered for trials with the Royal Engineers in September 1967. The vehicles carried two types of bridge, either the scissors type No 8 Bridge or the rigid No 9 Tank Bridge. The No 8 Tank Bridge could bridge a span of 75ft (22.9m), and was the longest AVLB in the world at the time of its introduction. The No 9 Tank Bridge, which was carried horizontally on the vehicle and then raised to swing vertically through 180 degrees, could cover a span of up to 40ft (12m). Both bridge types could support a weight of 80 tons.

The introduction of the Challenger Main Battle Tank in 1983 released quantities of surplus Chieftains for conversion to the AVRE role, replacing the Centurion AVRE vehicles, which now lacked the battlefield mobility to provide effective support for a battlegroup. An initial batch of twelve Chieftains had their turrets removed to provide enhanced mobility, even when laden with engineering equipment, and in 1989 a programme was set in motion to convert a further 48 vehicles. Known as the Chieftain Armoured Vehicle Royal Engineers (CHAVRE), each vehicle carried a winch and crane for recovery operations, together with rolls of trackway, fascines and stores. Equipment also included a dozer blade or mine plough.

The Chieftain ARV was fitted with winches capable of recovering any armoured vehicle then in service and a dozer blade that could be dug in and used as an anchor while the recovery operation was in progress. The first of 257 vehicles was delivered in 1974. (Norfolk Tank Museum)

A Chieftain bridgelayer pictured in company with a Spartan tracked armoured personnel carrier. (MoD)

The Chieftain in Service

United Kingdom

The Chieftain served in the armoured regiments of the British Army from 1965 to 1996, when the last examples were withdrawn. Total production for the British Army was 900 vehicles, mostly assigned to the 1st, 3rd and 4th Armoured Divisions of the British Army of the Rhine. These three armoured divisions formed the core element of 1(BR) Corps (HQ Bielefeld) and were based on twenty locations in Lower Saxony and North Rhine Westphalia. Each division had three brigades.

Chieftan Mk 11 00EB59 served with the British Army from 1967 to 1996, being first issued to the 17/21st Lancers (BAOR)

Above: A Chieftain MBT of the Royal Scots Dragoon Guards. (MoD)

Right: A Chieftain MBT preserved at the Ashchurch Military Depot near Tewskbury, Gloucestershire. (Wikimedia Commons)

Iran

After the United Kingdom, the main user of the Chieftain was Iran, which took delivery of 707 Mk 3P and Mk 5P, 187 FV4030, 41 ARV and 14 AVLB vehicles prior to the Islamic revolution of 1979. The FV4030 was an improved version of the Chieftain known as the Shir Iran 1, based on the Chieftain Mk 5 but with more fuel and additional protection. Iran also ordered 1,225 all new Shir Iran 2 tanks, production of which was about to begin at ROF Leeds when the revolution started and brought a halt to the project. The tanks were subsequently acquired by the British Army and, with modifications to fit them for European service, became the Challenger I.

Iraq

The Iraqi Army had between 50 and 75 Chieftains, all captured from Iran during the Iran–Iraq War of the 1980s. Most were upgraded with night vision equipment, reinforced armour and air conditioning.

Israel

In 1966, two Chieftains were shipped to Israel under conditions of strict secrecy to undergo comprehensive trials before further vehicles were to have been purchased 'off the shelf' prior to license manufacture by Israeli Military Industries (IMI). The deal was cancelled for political reasons in the aftermath of the 1967 Arab–Israeli War.

Jordan

In November 1989, Jordan placed an order with the UK for 274 Khalid MBTs, for delivery from 1981. The Khalid (Sword) was essentially a FV4030/2 Chieftain incorporating modifications to suit Jordanian requirements. These included a new power pack, comprising a Perkins Engines Company Condor V-12 1200 diesel, a David Brown Defence Equipment TN37 transmission and a new cooling system. Deliveries were completed in 1985. About 90 more Chieftains, captured from Iran, were acquired from Iraq.

Kuwait

Kuwait took delivery of 175 Chieftain Mk 5/2K tanks in 1976, 143 in 1989, and 20 in 1995. The Kuwaiti Chieftains were involved in a notable battle during the Iraqi invasion of 1990.

Oman

The Sultan of Oman's Armed Forces acquired twelve Chieftain Mk 7/2 tanks on loan from the British Army in August 1981, a further fifteen new-build vehicles being added to the end of 1985.

Iran placed a massive order for 1,225 Shir Iran 1 tanks, but the Islamic revolution caused its cancellation. (Tank Museum)

One of the 50-plus Iranian Chieftains captured by Iraq in the wake of the Iran–Iraq War and used by the Iraqi forces. (US Army)

Jordan's Khalid MBT sporting a distinctive camouflage scheme. (Source unknown)

Allies and Adversaries

THE CHIEFTAIN'S CONTEMPORARIES

Allies

In the early weeks of 1968, a Chieftain MBT was assigned to the Detachement ter Beproeving van Voertuigen (Vehicle Testing Detachment) of the Royal Netherlands Army for comparative trials with West Germany's new Leopard I MBT. The Leopard was eventually selected largely because of the Chieftain's poor construction quality, especially the engine, which leaked so much oil that the engine compartment turned black.

There was to be no repeat of the success enjoyed by the Chieftain's predecessor, the Centurion, which had been selected to equip the majority of the armoured divisions of European NATO and Canada. Instead, the Leopard I main battle tank, alongside the Chieftain, was to become an extremely important element of NATO's land warfare defence during the most dangerous years of the Cold War.

The Leopard project was initiated in 1956, the object being to develop a new AFV to replace the Bundeswehr's M47 and M48 tanks, which were becoming obsolescent. The requirement called for a vehicle that would withstand hits from a 20mm anti-tank gun and be able to operate in an environment contaminated by nuclear, chemical or biological warfare. The gun selected for its main armament was the British L7A3 105mm weapon. In June 1957 Germany and France signed an agreement to develop the new tank, known initially as the Standard-Panzer. Two German and one French design teams were invited to submit proposals, each team producing two prototypes. Italy joined the development programme in 1958.

Testing of the various prototypes began in 1960, and it was the design submitted by Porsche that was selected, although some changes to the original design were made before it was accepted for production. These included a new cast turret and several hull changes to raise the rear deck in order to

The problems experienced during the Chieftain's early development phase caused potential customers to lose faith in British tank designers. This image shows two Leopard tanks of the Royal Norwegian Army on manoeuvres in the snow. (Royal Norwegian Army)

make a roomier engine compartment. An optical range-finder system was also added.

The first batch of production Leopard 1 tanks was built by Krauss-Maffei of Munich between September 1955 and June 1966. The next three batches comprised the Leopard 1A1 model, which included a new gun stabilisation system. The Leopard 1A1 was subjected to various upgrades in the 1970s. Follow-on models were the Leopard 1A2, with a more heavily armoured turret; the 1A3, with a new welded turret; the 1A4, with a new computerized fire control system; the 1A5, which featured a completely new turret; and the 1A6, with additional armour and a 120mm gun.

The Leopard 1 was exported to, or manufactured in, 12 countries, the biggest customer being Italy, which acquired 920. The other customers were Australia (90), Belgium (132), Brazil (240), Canada (114), Chile (unspecified), Denmark (330), Greece (335), the Netherlands (unspecified), Norway (172) and Turkey (307). The Bundeswehr employed 724, which were progressively replaced by the Leopard 2. During the Cold War, the Leopard and the British Chieftain would have borne the brunt of any tank battle that might have developed on the North German plain, and would have played a decisive part in blunting any Soviet offensive. The commonality between the armies using the Leopard in this sector – German, Belgian and Dutch – would have been an important factor.

The Chieftain's American contemporary was the M60, the last in the line of US main battle tanks that began with the M46. Its development began in response to intelligence, received in 1957, that the Russians were developing a new medium tank, the T-62, which was armed with a 115mm gun that would make it superior to the American M48. The simplest solution was to fit the existing M48 with a more powerful engine and a new gun, the chosen weapon being the British 105mm L7. With these improvements the modified tank, originally designated M68, went into production in 1959 and was deployed operationally in 1960. Re-designated M60, its production run (all variants) eventually totalled 15,000 units. The first prototypes and early production machines were completed at the Chrysler Corporation's Delaware Defense Plant, but from 1960 production switched to the Detroit Tank Plant, also operated by Chrysler (later taken over by General Dynamics). Production ceased in 1987.

The M60 underwent various upgrades during its operational life, the first in 1963, when the M60A1 appeared with a larger and better-designed turret, improved armour and more efficient shock-absorbers. The next variant, the M60A2, featured a redesigned low-profile turret with a commander's machine gun cupola on top, giving the commander a good view and field of fire while remaining protected. It was also armed with a 152mm calibre main gun similar to that of the M551 Sheridan, which was able to fire the Shillelagh gun-launched anti-tank missile as well as normal rounds. The M60A2 was abandoned after a relatively short time and most were rebuilt to the standard of the next variant, the M60A3. This incorporated a number of technological advances such as a new rangefinder and ballistic computer and a turret stabilisation system. All American M60s were upgraded to this standard.

France's armoured contribution to the defence of western Europe was the AMX-30 Main Battle Tank. Development of the AMX-30 started in the mid-1950s in response to a French Army Requirement for a new, indigenous main battle tank to replace the ageing AFVs of American origin and Second World War vintage. The design of the tank, developed by the Atelier de Construction d'Issy-les-Moulineaux, made no attempt to produce a vehicle that carried very heavy armour protection; instead, design philosophy favoured a vehicle with less heavy armour, but with high

An M60A3 MBT on display in Lake Charles, Louisiana. The M60A3 incorporated a number of technological advances such as a new rangefinder and ballistic computer and a turret stabilisation system. All American M60s were upgraded to this standard. (US Army)

Continues to page 49

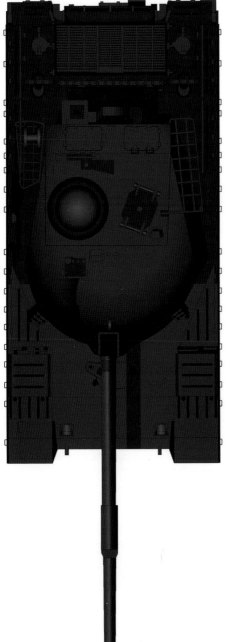

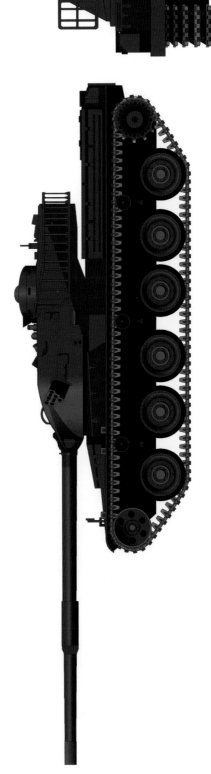

A pre-production Chieftain built by the Royal Ordnance Factory at Barnbow, Leeds. The commander's cupola is smaller than that fitted to production models. Note the absence of protective track guards, or 'Bazooka Plates' as they were known.

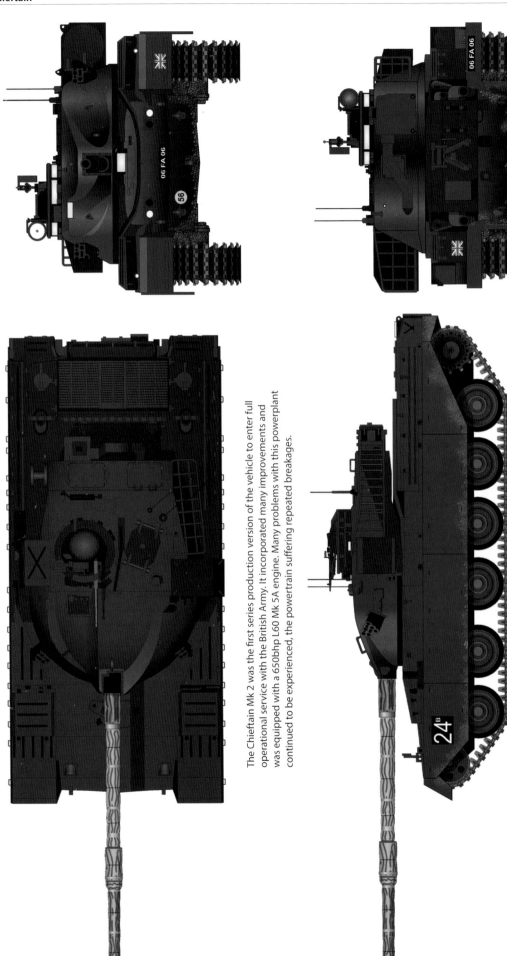

The Chieftain Mk 2 was the first series production version of the vehicle to enter full operational service with the British Army. It incorporated many improvements and was equipped with a 650bhp L60 Mk 5A engine. Many problems with this powerplant continued to be experienced, the powertrain suffering repeated breakages.

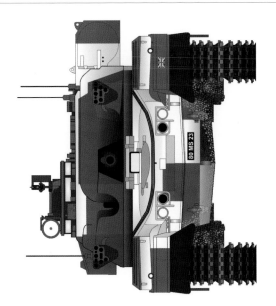

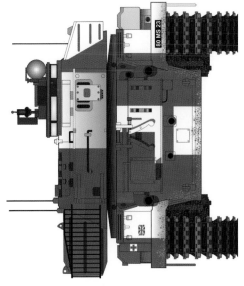

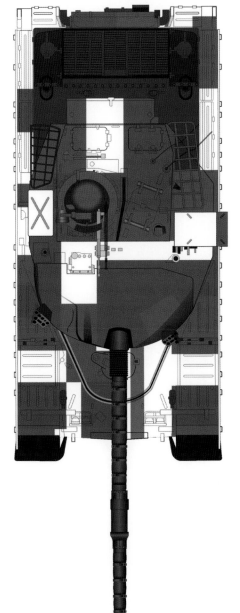

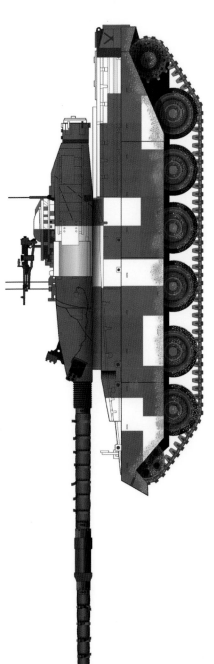

A Chieftain Mk 3 of the Berlin Brigade, sporting its distinctive urban camouflage, adopted after much experimentation to develop a scheme that would blend in well with the colours and angular features of streets and buildings. The camouflage proved very effective, the vehicles being difficult to spot, especially from the air.

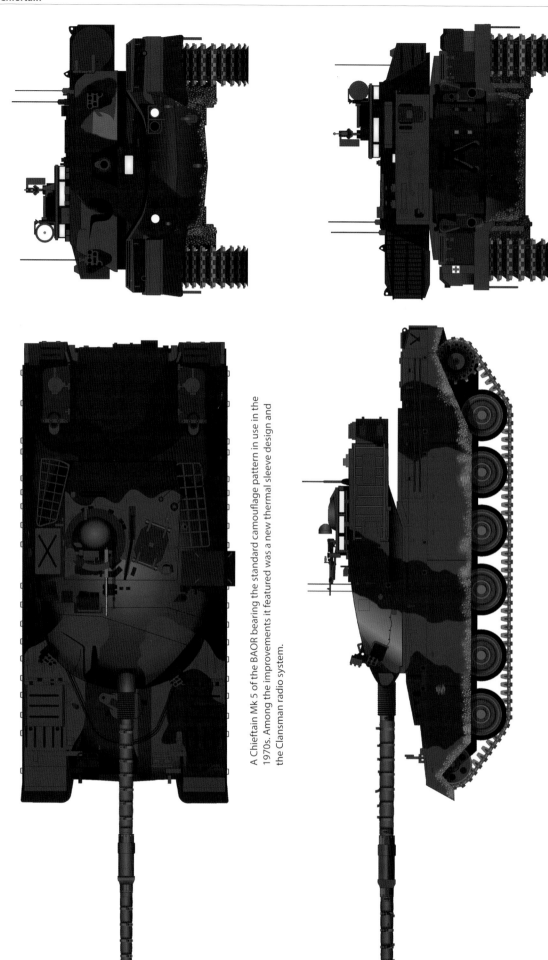

A Chieftain Mk 5 of the BAOR bearing the standard camouflage pattern in use in the 1970s. Among the improvements it featured was a new thermal sleeve design and the Clansman radio system.

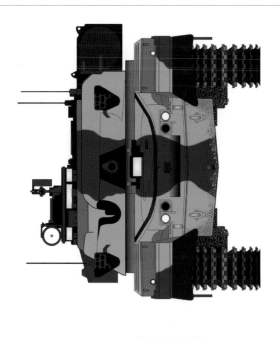

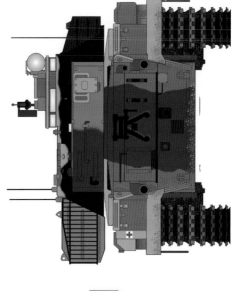

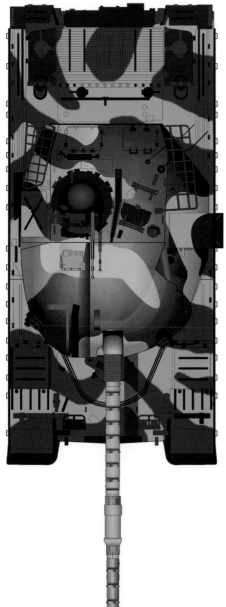

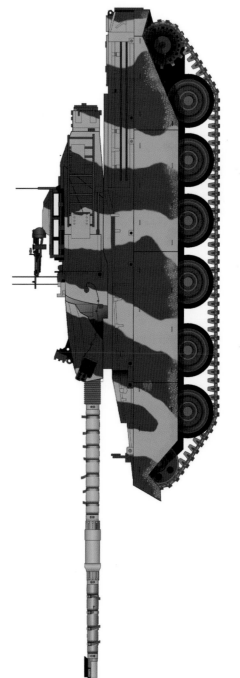

The Chieftain Mk 10, seen here, was an upgrade of the Mk 9 and the first to incorporate the Stillbrew armoured protection package at the front of the turret.

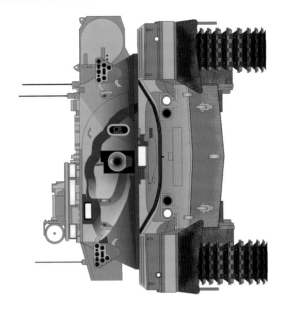

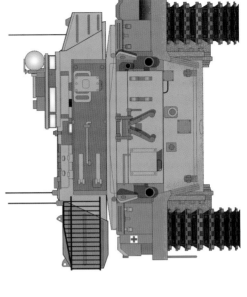

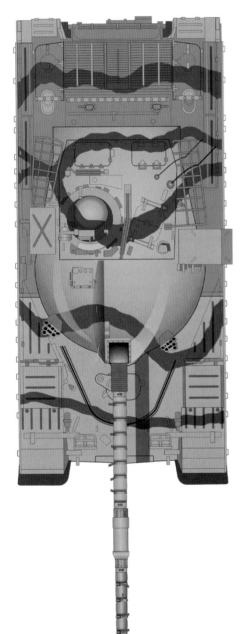

One of the Chieftain Mk 10 tanks acquired by the Sultan of Oman's Armed Forces. These were new-build vehicles, a batch of 15 being delivered by the end of 1985.

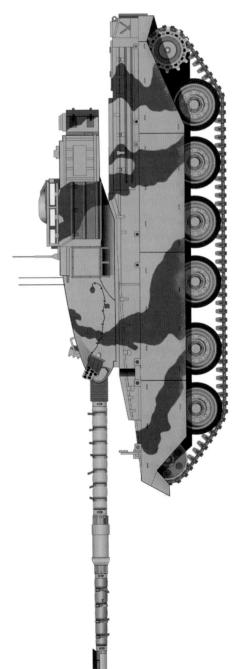

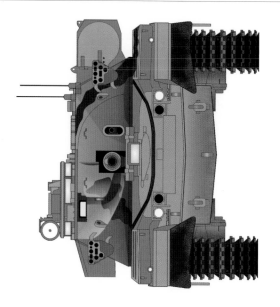

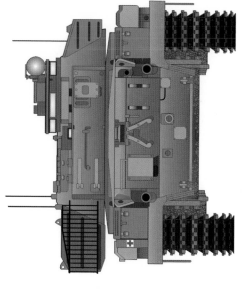

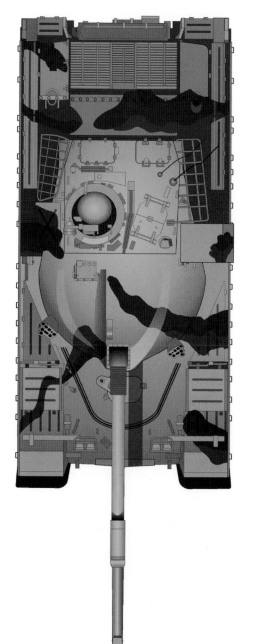

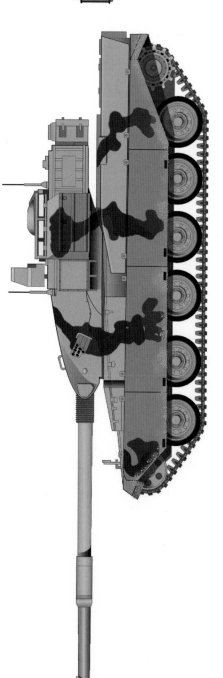

After the United Kingdom, the main user of the Chieftain was Iran, which took delivery of 707 Mk 3P and Mk 5P, 187 FV4030, 41 ARV and 14 AVLB vehicles prior to the Islamic revolution of 1979. The FV4030 was an improved version of the Chieftain known as the Shir Iran 1, based on the Chieftain Mk 5 but with more fuel and additional protection.

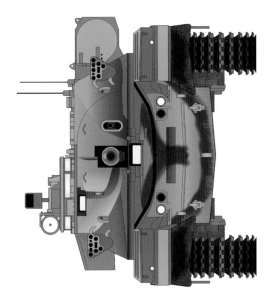

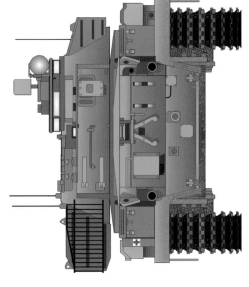

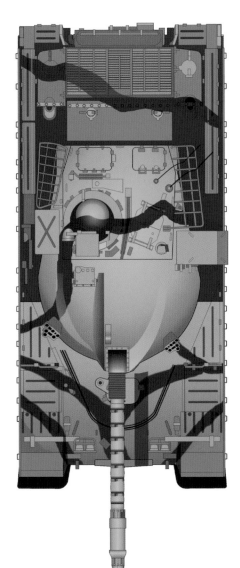

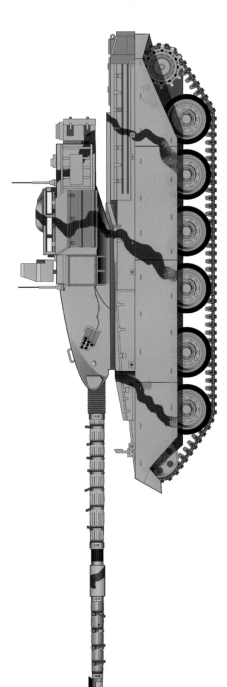

In November 1989, Jordan placed an order with the UK for 274 Khalid (Sword) MBTs, for delivery from 1981. The Khalid (Sword) was essentially a FV4030/2 Chieftain incorporating modifications to suit Jordanian requirements.

CHIEFTAIN MK 5
British Mainland
1/35 Scale
Robert Bausch

This is the 1/35 scale Tamiya kit of the Chieftain Mk 5. It was built stock, out of the box. Some folded up blankets/tarps were added to fit in the stowage racks. The dust protector where the main gun protrudes from the turret was also added. At the time the model was built it was the only kit available in 1/35 scale, reviews suggest it is probably more similar to the Mk 3 than the Mk 5. No aftermarket parts were used. Gunze Sangyo acrylic paints were used. (Model and photographs by Robert Bausch www.bauschdesign.com to see more of Robert Bausch's models and art.)

The tarps in the stowage racks on the turret rear were made of folded bathroom tissue (like Kleenex) and then airbrushed in several colors. The canvas dust protector where the main gun comes out of the turret mantlet is made in a similar way to the tarps, though I used a slightly thicker paper there and it was painted by hand. This was one of the most difficult parts of the build.

The vehicle registration number 04 EB 35 is on the front of the hull and on the right rear fender. This number appears to be in a range that might include either a Chieftain Mk 3 or 5. The white triangle symbols on the searchlight housing and stowage bins are probably unit markings (Squadron A), but I was not able to find out any more info about them. The yellow disc with 56 in black on the front of the hull is the bridging disc weight marking.

3/63 on the right front fender may be a unit nunber and appears front and rear too. Al Capone is the tank's nickname; the radio call sign on the NBC housing at the rear of the turret is 12A. The red AF symbol on the left turret rear means the engine in this tank has anti-freeze.

The main gun barrel with thermal sleeve was painted by hand, as were the figures of the tank crewmen.

Model and photographs by Robert Bausch. Visit his website at www.bauschdesign.com to see more of Robert Bausch's scale models and art.

CHIEFTAIN MK 5
British Army of the Rhine
1978–82
1/35 Scale
Brian Richardson

Takom's Chieftain Mk 5/5P no. 2027 released in 2015 is a very comprehensive, detailed kit, straight from the box with seven different options on the decal sheet including BATUS, Berlin Brigade, Iranian and Kuwait versions. I've gone for a British Army of the Rhine (BAOR) Mk 5 variant from the late 70s early 80s using a combination of Takom and Tamiya decals.

Further cammo netting was made from surgical gauze soaked in diluted PVA / white glue with fine oregano sprinkled while the glue was still wet. Some additional webbing to the barrel was achieved with short lengths of sewing cotton super glued hanging down with more oregano.

To increase the level of detail even further I've added Voyager Model PE 35759, Eduard padlocks and side skirt loops from their ED35771 set and a Cast Off gun tube from their CR 051 kit. Takom have provided a sheet of photo etch for the turret basket, engine deck screens and a few other details which are quite adequate but Voyager's are much finer and more detailed.

Squadron green putty took care of the many welds and copper wire together with thin solder cabled the headlights, fire suppression handles and replaced the moulded-on cabling for the turret-mounted grenade launchers.

Also both turret and hull stowage bin drains are missing from the kit. These were added with short lengths of 0.6mm brass tube, normally these were fitted with plugs but I decided to leave them open. The bins were filled with a variety of boxes, jerry cans and packs from the spares box. The crew figures also came from a variety of spares.

Fortunately Voyager also supply a length of braided copper wire to replace the kit's plastic parts. It's nearly impossible to remove the mould line without destroying the detail. A couple of small details I picked from studying reference photos are the holes in the end of the engine deck's rubber bumpers, these are kit parts A24, 25 and 26. An easy fix with a 1mm drill bit. After priming Tamiya XF-65 Field Grey was sprayed followed with XF-69 Nato Black. Various enamels and oils took care of the weathering.

CHIEFTAIN MK 5

3rd Royal Tank Regiment, British Army of the Rhine
1/35 Scale
Anthony Leone

Awarded gold in the Advanced Category at the Armorcon (AMPs East Regional Model Show).

Based in Paderborn Germany, 'Cambrai' was the CO's tank of the Headquarters Squadron, 3rd Royal Tank Regiment (RTR) c. 1979–1986. As C Battalion of the Tank Corps, in November 1917 the regiment first saw action in the massive tank assault at the Battle of Cambrai. As soon as I found the image of 'Cambrai' with its distinctive lobed-camo pattern, I knew my subject. BAOR camo schemes are typically thick black bands over green, this scheme provided an interesting alternative – reminiscent of the circular patterned British camo during the war, which was often referred to as the Mickey Mouse pattern. The kit featured here is the Takom Chieftain Mk 5P. Generally speaking, the Takom kit is a solid offering. It can be built as either a standard issue Mk 5 or as an Mk 5P, the P designating the versions sold to either Iran or Kuwait. The Takom kit comes with a well-done instruction booklet and a nice little accordion fold brochure featuring paint schemes and markings offered with the kit.

Painting and weathering of this build was undertaken with my usual course of action which includes a heavy dose of intuition and a mad combo of Steve Zaloga and Mike Rinaldi-inspired techniques. I use Tamiya paints for basecoat airbrushing, Vallejo and Testors Model Master for details, Winsor & Newton and Holbein artist oils for weathering and pigments.

In order to capture the lobed-camo scheme, I used the few references I found online which depicted the camo pattern of one side of the tank hull and a turret side and rear view. I loosely penciled this pattern on the tank and hand-painted the outlines with Tamiya Nato Black. Using a fine needle on my airbrush I managed to fill the pattern without too much overspray.

A last minute decision was to cut out a panel of the side skirts, such as photos of Cambrai show. I was a bit apprehensive to do this, as I was happy with the paint job thus far, and if I messed up the cut I'd be sunk. I took the risk with my trusty razor saw and I am glad I did. The open panel adds viewable detail to the running gear, which are otherwise concealed by the side-skirts. Cutting the panels after they were painted helped lend a natural appearance to the camo as well.

In order to model Cambrai, I needed to create a small set of custom decals, as there are no aftermarket options that I was able to find. I've been wanting to try my hand at custom decals for some time and this was the perfect opportunity. Custom dry transfer decals are expensive, but can be made worthwhile if you gang decals for several builds on the standard sheet sizes offered.

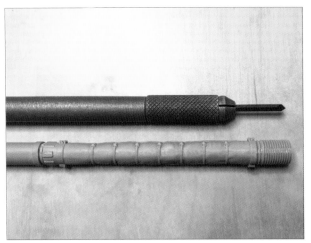

The barrel is a two-part moulded assembly. This is something I'd typically replace with a turned aftermarket metal barrel, however, the Chieftain barrel features the distinct thermal sleeves, so I decided to make do with the kit's parts. The fit was very good, however, I pulled out details on the barrel with one of my favorite detail implements – a scratchboard tool set that I've had since I was a pre-teen art student. There are various points one can insert into an X-acto type of handle. The points allow me to deepen moulded seams for a more realistic effect and better help paint washes catch the detail.

The kit comes supplied with a nice set of PE screens for the air vents on the rear deck. Some are covered under the large overhang on the turret, but the detail is very good.

Figure options on the market for post-war British tank crews are thin at best. Those that are available are expensive and don't feature in-tank poses. Royal tankies wore black jumpsuits, similar to Second World War panzer crews. I found that with some careful sanding, a set of Dragon figures (German Panzer Crew LAH Division, Russia 1943 / Dragon 6214) from my stash would do the trick. With some altering of arm positions, adding distinctive British name badges and a set of superb Hornet heads, I had a Chieftain commander and loader.

Headlamp wiring was scratch-built using brass wire. I find these additions really add a bit of fine visual noise and realism to the final presentation of the model.

Some parts of the kit required a little added detail. Here I added some detailing around the commander's search light and I built out a grab handle for the turret-mounted machine gun.

The Chieftain features huge turret baskets for stowage and most references see them filled to brim with gear. However, I decided to leave them open to show off the photo-etch details of the basket screens. They're quite like fine pieces of jewelry and lend a nice fidelity to the overall look of the build.

Bottom left: The front mud guards were thinned and bent to better represent a more flexible material.

Bottom right: The kit comes with a nice set of PE parts. However, the PE grab handles are flat. So I replaced those on the turret hatch with round brass wire.

CHIEFTAIN MK 11

BRITISH ARMY OF THE RHINE
1992
1/35 Scale
Morgen Violet-Harris

This kit is the Takom Mk.11, finished in black and green camouflage, located in Germany, 1992. The box includes seven main sprues in grey plastic including one duplicate for the wheels and suspension, 200+ individual track links, six sprues of rubber pads for the tracks, one clear sprue, upper and lower hull parts, upper and lower turret, one sheet of photo-etch, two polly caps, a soft plastic material simulates the canvas dust cover for the main gun, decals, a 13-page manual across 22 steps and a fold-out A5 leaflet with five different marking options. Overall the kit went together fairly easily and following the kit instructions should keep the builder out of trouble.

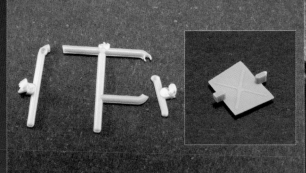
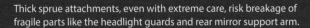

Thick sprue attachments, even with extreme care, risk breakage of fragile parts like the headlight guards and rear mirror support arm.

The road wheels consist of five parts: this produces a lot of time consuming clean-up but does accurately portray the correct shape.

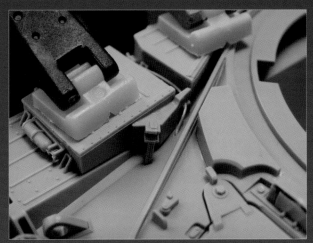

No cable is supplied to attach the handle for the hull fire extinguishers so I built mine out of stretched sprue.

Modellers often leave the tracks until later as this makes painting and weathering easier, I suggest following the instructions due to the very small gap between upper hull and running gear which makes (re-)threading the previously assembled tracks difficult and risks damaged or broken parts.

A small photo-etch support arm is attached between the headlight guard and splash guard, care should be taken to get the alignment of the bend in the correct direction. Barrel detail can be achieved with careful assembly of the kit barrel and painting.

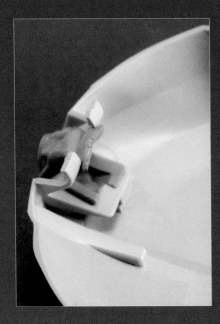

Due to alignment grooves moulded into the 'gun mask' it is easier to fit this piece to the upper turret and then attach the lower turret section, leaving the fitting of the main barrel until after the upper and lower turret halves are joined.

Careful assembly leaves turret hatches usable (the drivers hatch much be selected open or closed), I didn't detail-paint them as I had no crew, but the option is there if the builder so wishes)

Detail provided inside and out of the rangefinder housing.

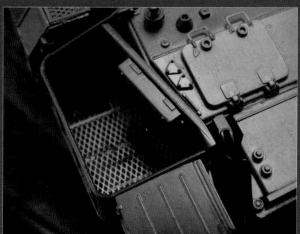

The kit photo-etch fits perfectly and helps bring out the details.

The completed model was primed with Tamiya Liquid Surface Primer and then painted with Gunze Aqueous H423 Dark Green and Tamiya XF-69 NATO Black. Most photos showed very low wear or paint chipping but often had a good layer of dirt or mud up the side skirts so I used this as my guide for weathering. I first applied a light filter of Humbrol 94 thinned to about 95% thinner–5% paint to give an overall dusted look, then coated the lower hull with Ammo of Mig's 'Dry Steppe Medium Density Mud Splashes' medium and carefully applied same to the wheels and tracks using reference photos as a guide. Weathering was then finished by spraying Tamiya XF-57 Buff and about 85-90% thinner–10-15% paint at 15 PSI over both horizontal and vertical surfaces until the desired look was achieved.

Through use of careful sanding, panting and a light wash, detail really shows. The light wash helps bring out some of the details while in keeping with the light weathering most Chieftains received.

Tamiya was first to release kits on this modern British battle tank, with four releases starting in 1965 and ending 12 years later. All four are in 1/25 scale. The Tamiya Chiftain Mk 5 that is currently available is 1/35 scale. Airfix released a Chieftain in 1970 which it has reboxed eight times and made available in 1/72 ans 1/76 scale. The last release was in 2005 and although these older versions are still around there is nothing in the modern Airfix branding available on its own website or otherwise. In 1982 MPC collaborated with Airfix and released a Chieftain in 1/76 scale. Academy came on board in the late 1970s with a Mk. 5 which was re-released a couple of years later. It collaborated with Minicraft in 1986, reboxing its Mk. 5 and then reboxed it again as a stand-alone Academy product at the end of that decade, however, it was no longer available

at the time of writing. Takom has five Chieftains in its collection, all of which were released from 2015 onward. Meng Models made a single kit available in 2016 of the Mk. 10 and AFV Club released a Mk. 6 in 2016. However, it seems the AFV Club model never materialized, some modellers say it was a hoax and others that the timing was bad due to Takom's releases and they therefore pulled out. There box art but no model it appears. There are four additional Chieftain kits, now quite old but still available: two are made in Japan, one by Matuo Kasten, a 1/144 Chieftain Mk. 5 and one by Micro Ace, a 1/48 Chieftain remote control tank. Britain's Cromwell Models has a 1/72 Chieftain Mk. 4 and the American Winneco (of Palmer Plastics) has a 1/72 Chieftain Medium Tank. Matador Models also have two Chieftains in their catalogue.

CROMWELL MODELS

Cromwell models offers a range of 1/72 scale resin Chieftain models which, as can be seen in the photos, all break down in much the same way. Their catalogue includes: Chieftain MK2 MBT (72110), Chieftain MK4 - Israeli Spec. (72245), Chieftain MK11 MBT (72246), Chieftain Burlington MBT (72256), Chieftain MK2. GBT 155 (72257), Chieftain Marksman (72258) and a Chieftain MK10 (72265).

1) 72110
2) 72265
3) 72246
4) 72258
5) 72257

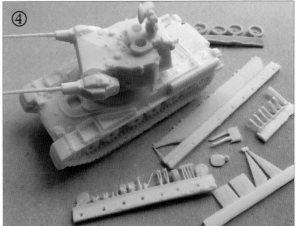

This Chieftain Mk 10 kit is cast in cream resin and requires minimal clean up and construction. No instructions or paint guides are included so the modeller will have to rely on their own references. Super glue works well on resin kits and is quick and easy. This model is primed with a few light coats of an automotive acrylic primer, it was then painted in a generic Batus camouflage scheme and does not represent any specific vehicle. To add depth a mixture of enamels are airbrushed for the main colours with oil paint washes. A light dry brush brings out the raised detail, and light weathering was added to give the impression of an operational vehicle. The model is completed by adding aerials from stretched sprue and a light coat of matt varnish.

(Model and images courtesy of Neil McConnachie, Creative Time Wasting)

TAMIYA

Tamiya's only current kit is a British Army Chieftain Mk 5 in 1/35 scale. The sprues indicate a copyright year of 1975 but even so the detail is good and although there are mould seams around most of the parts, this is easily sanded or scraped off and there is little flash and the ejector pin marks are on the inside of the parts so won't be visible after assembly. However this also applies to the inside of the hatches, so those of course are visible and will need attending to. The .50 cal and two 7.62mm machine guns are moulded solid and will need hollowing out if you want to use the kit parts and no gun mantlet is provided. The area around the mantlet will also need attention due to a seam that affects the turret shape. (Watch the seam on the gun tube too.) The slightly rough cast texture on the turret and hull works well and the fabric texture on the thermal sleeve of the 120mm machine gun is nicely done. This kit used to be motorized so the lower hull still leaves place for the batteries, this will cause unwanted light shining into the interior. The kit includes three half-body figures: two for the turret and one is the driver, they are cast in realistic poses. The decals provide for three markings: on manoeuvres in Canada in dark green (XF-61) with a flat green (XF-5) camouflage pattern; on manoeuvres in England in the same colour scheme and one stationed in West Germany in overall dark green (XF-61). Like the Takom kits, the Tamiya kit is readily available but is cheaper although not as detailed. It builds into a fine model.

The above review pertains to the kit as it comes out the box. However, all modellers will know that, depending on their level of skill and experience, the final build can look very different from what the the original kit builds into. The Chieftain in these photographs started life as this Tamiya kit but underwent extensive correction and additions, not to mention artistic flair (aftermarket products used include Friul tracks, a Cast Off resin conversion set andan Eduard PE set). Mike Griffin explains some of the steps involved in modifying this Tamiya kit in order to build this outstanding Chieftain Mk 5 in service with the Islamic Republic of Iran Army during the Iran–Iraq War of 1980–1988.

Early modifications include routing the block face of the wading rail to create a channel; removing the moulded front turret splashguard behind the driver's periscope; expanding rear-most transmission grills from three to four and correcting the angle and pitch; filled in motorization holes in hull bottom (1); removed the moulded-on rear wading rail and added back the bottom channel leg; removed all the moulded-on skirt attachment brackets from the fender edges; removed front fenders (2).

During assembly further alterations were made: the hull side extensions and weld beads were added; the grab handles have been removed flush to the grills and the cross frame for the center transmission grills have been added as well as two .010 outer grill edge strips for a proper fit (3); the fit at the nose is poor, the upper hull nose angle is different to the lower requiring reshaping; lightening holes to the longitudinal depression stop rails have been added; the PE set front stowage bins were used but their lines are replaced with wire; the casting is offset and the detail is soft on the lift rings and tow hooks (4); the fit of the bins at the back is poor and required much repositioning (5); repositioned

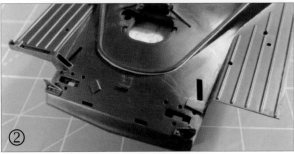

rear lifting eyes and removed the small moulded-on fitting to the right of the travel lock; fitted Cast Off's exhaust pipes by cutting the integral resin base flange off and correcting the pipe mounting angle; Eduard PE set engine deck screens were used for the forward panels and one of the inner rear panels and modified two others for the outer panels, cutting to size, adding the 'notches' and forming the frame with styrene strip (1); more styrene strip was used to create raised bands at housing ends to create bogey unit detail (the bogeys also suffer from major mould seam/offsets requiring scraping and sanding) and the kit's side skirt lower mounting struts were replaced with styrene and brass assemblies; much tweaking has been done to the struts, wheels and rollers to adjust the alignment and increase clearance (2).

These are the basic add-on fixtures and kit revisions, using parts of the Cast Off resin conversion set and styrene stock: replace cupola/periscopes with larger diameter/angled scopes similar to Challenger; add rectangular relief valve behind cupola; replace NBC pack with No.6 Mk 2 unit (you may replace the turret bustle rear panel with styrene sheet or remove moulded details from the kit part to receive the pack as it is off-center to the right for side fixture); add box for aerial tuning – right front with added styrene bolts and bottom plate; add weld beads at side panel joint, radio box, lift lugs; add two blocks with threaded holes below mantlet; add searchlight power conduit – left side back; detail commander's sight; add searchlight mounting blocks/brackets: two front, one back; drill hole at spotlight fixing ring, add ring: top front, right of cupola; remove locator shelf and add stand-off brackets and back panel to commander's stowage bin; replace antennae base(s) with Clansman type: Challenger (for this Iranian subject I only did the one atop the control box and show cover plates for the other positions); reposition rear lift lugs from vertical to angled forward; remove kit pins and reposition left rear side box and add stand-off brackets.

Wrapping up the turret with various PE and scratch detailing, included the following items of note: added mantlet and coax MG dust cover using tissue/white glue. Note the cover perimeter frame configuration needs to be corrected with the upper portions replaced/added; replaced kit cheek MG port/cover with scratch item; enlarged the left stowage basket and screen insert – extended to end of searchlight box and corrected the attachments; reworked the front right turret shape and added some material to create a much shallower hard edged 'crescent' on the vertical face; detailed the commander's spot light and MG; added rear lift cable guide to the bustle corners using styrene shapes; added the large ammo box for the right basket. (3&4)

The Friulmodel white metal tracks should be assembled a bag at a time and fit the kit drive sprocket nicely. With their side skirt mounting arms, the bogeys were then affixed to the hull (5). The kit barrel is a little undersized and not a very good rendition of the thermal sleeve so I decided to use the two-piece styrene L11 gun from the Tamiya Challenger I. I omitted the muzzle reference mirror as photographs couldn't definitively show its location. I modified the thermal sleve to show some stretching, twisting and a torn strap. The front clamp is further toward the end of the barrel and I cut the kit end cap in half and completed the clamp where the omitted mirror was.

Some fixtures have been left off as battle damage and for artistic effect, they could allow even more detailing. Items of note include: the main gun barrel has the strap ends made from two layers of Tamiya Tape; the stowage consists of a tarp made from wine bottle foil, the scratch ammo box, resin water cans, a small flimsy from the spares and AFV Club M19A1 ammo cans, often used for 7.62 ammo (6); the tracks' sag was removed by going to a metal axle, gluing everything stiff and placing pins under the tracks, like making sag for rubber bands in reverse.

⑤

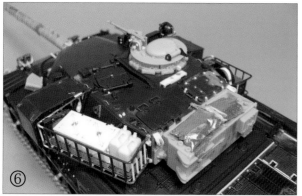

⑥

⑦

As a primer/base coat I chose Tamiya XF-60, Dark Yellow. It is darker than the official colour but it works as a foundation and reveals any minor body work needed. Next, a darker 'shadow wash' with artist oil was applied and then back to acrylic with lighter general shades (7). The upper hull's paint work consisted of: a light oil wash mix of burnt umber/payne's grey/ivory black; an over spray of Tamiya Buff, varying the intensity to create some highlights; another general light brush wash of the above oil mix. The Commander's MG is semi-gloss black, detailed and weathered a bit. For the main gun barrel, the thermal sleeve is Tamiya XF62 Olive Drab lightened with yellow and Khaki, the 'dust shroud' is Nato Black and the straps are Khaki. Finally, I weathered the lower hull, paint and the tires, pulled off the mask tape and painted the details and tracks.

Some final comments on painting: the headlights are MV lenses; tow cable – Karaya, painted tan with washes of burnt umber and Paynes Grey; main periscope lenses are 35mm film with some Sand powder; cupola lenses are painted black, as the many wipers were moulded in the resin part; markings are decals for a 1/72 Iranian jet fighter; the tracks were painted flat black, then a heavy wash of Tamiya Dark Brown using Tamiya Thinner, then a wash of burnt sienna oil; track pads are Tamiya Dark Grey; then an overall heavy application of MM Powders Sand, fixed with mineral spirits. The body was highlighted with Tamiya Buff. Some details such as the fire extinguishing equipment were painted the body colour, supposing this could have been done, as I like the overall look better after trying them picked out with green/red. Nato black was used for the tires and for scrapes and scuffs, done with a tiny brush and some small dry-brush stippling. Another targeted brush wash of burnt umber and then a wash of dust with an oil mixture of white, raw umber and Paynes Grey, with a small brush for pin wash and a large one for general dust; rust stains are burnt sienna wash; exhaust stains are black pastel.

The heavy weathering helps bring out the model's many corrections and added details and tells the story of the long war with Iraq and this tank's life in the desert.

TAKOM

Takom kits are all available in 1/35 scale. Its range is fairly extensive and includes a Chieftain Marksman Spaag, a Mk. 2, a Mk. 5/5P, A Mk. 10 and a Mk. 11. The latter three have the same basic hull, over 60% of the parts are similar; the majority of the fittings such as the commander's cupola, gunner's hatch, smoke dischargers and the sighting unit on the top of the turret are shared between all marks but turret, fixture and fitting changes differentiate them. The Mk. 5/5P is a 2-in-1 kit, allowing you to build the 5 or the 5P that was sold to the Iranians before the revolution. From the box you can build one of six examples: Unknown unit BATUS 1991; two Iranian Mk.5Ps from the Battle of Shalamche; Iranian 5P recaptured from Iraqi army by Iranian Revolutionary Guards Corp; Iranian 5P Army Day Parade, Tehran 2001; Kuwaiti Mk.5K Martyr's Brigade, Operation Desert Storm; D Squadron, 4/7th Dragoon Guards, Berlin. The Mk. 10 uses different turret parts to accommodate the Stillbrew armour package, and has a large insert on the left side to get the shapes right. It is where the Stillbrew package sits that a new fully open basket of similar construction to the earlier one hangs from the side. Four colour and marking options are available for this mark: Rhe Zombie Tank, Atlanta; A Squadron, 1 RTRm, BATRUS 1991; Hard Target Chieftain at Warcop range; C Squadron, 14.20 King's Royal Hussars, berlin 1988–91. For ultimate accuracy on the Zombie tank you'll need to check the remaining equipment fit and replicate some additional stencils on both the sides, front and rear of the tank. The Mk. 11 adds two small covered stowage boxes aft of the open baskets and favours the TOGS unit over the searchlight. This builds up into two linked boxes from a fair number of parts with a clear lens at the front if you decide to open the protective cover. A small PE mesh vent on the top rear finishes off the detail. Five decal options are available: Unknown unit, BATUS; A Squadron, 1 RTR Tofrek Barracks, Germany 1992; twounit markings are available for the 5th Inniskilling Dragoo Guards, BATUS Canada; Royal Scots Dragoon Guards. These Takom kits have put the outdated, after-market product heavy Tamiya kit to pasture. This is modern tooling of an iconic British Main Battle Tank.

Modeller Anthony Leone says on the Takom Mk 5P kit: The engineering quality of the kit falls somewhere between that of a Dragon and Tamiya offering. In general, the fit of parts was good, the exception being the road wheels and bogie mounts, in which the fit tolerance was so tight between the road wheels and the axle pins that a couple of the pins broke while test fitting. This is not a problem if you are to paint the build after complete assembly, but I tend to paint the running gear in various phases that requires them to be removed a couple of times over the course of the build. The mould detail was generally quite good, with only a few sections needing some scratch-built fidelity (such as the commander's searchlight, some machine gun details and headlamp wiring). To be fair, I believe these type of parts are challenging to mold, so Takom most likely did the best they could without over-complicating the parts. And I do like a little bit of scratch building – it's model-making after all. Typically a builder of WW2 subjects, the Takom kit was a pleasant introduction to post-war and more modern vehicles.

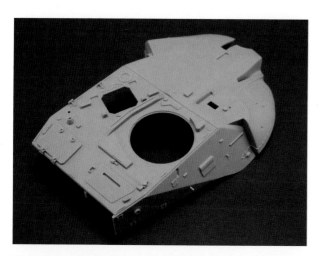

The new turret for the Mk 10/11with thicker armour around the front and multiple parts.

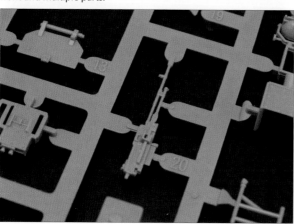

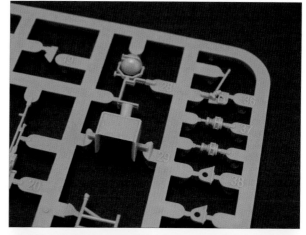

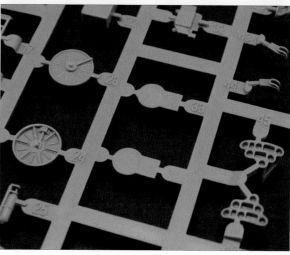

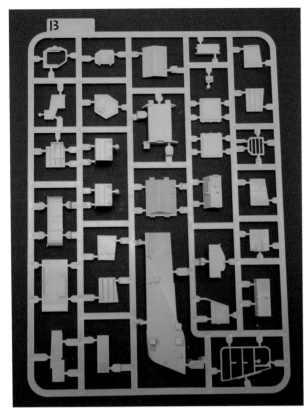

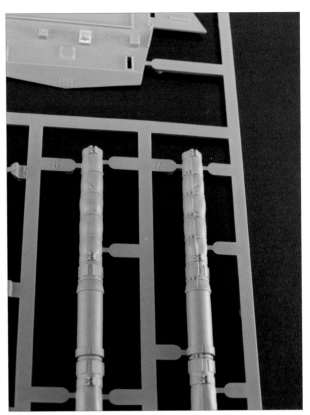

The Mk 11 gets a new square shaped TOGS searchlight on Sprue B that also includes the turret side. Also spotted are a couple of new turret basket parts.

Takom's detail in their range of Chieftain kits has excited modellers, here the gun barrel moulding can clearly be seen.

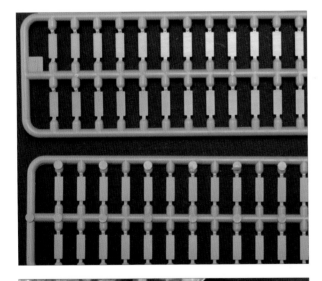

Shows the details achieved by having four parts to each outside half of the road wheels.

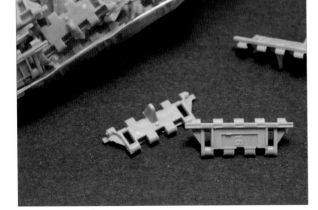

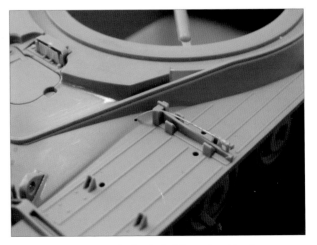

The rubber tracks re supplied separate of the ndividual links, resulting in ease of track painting for the modeller.

The kit supplied the handles for the hull fire extinguisher but strangely no cable, use stretched sprue and drill a small hole for fitting

Continues from page 16

An M60A3 winds its way through the narrow streets of a typical German town as part of an armoured convoy. (US Army)

speed and manoeuvrability and a main armament that was sufficiently advanced and accurate to kill an opponent with a first shot. The first prototypes were completed in 1960 and series production began in 1966, over 3,500 AMX-30s and variants subsequently being completed for the home and export markets. The French Army took delivery of 387 AMX-30s and 659 AMX-30B2s, the latter introducing a number of improvements including an integrated fire-control system incorporating a laser rangefinder and a low-light TV system, and an upgraded automotive system including a new transmission. In common with the Chieftain, early production AMX-30 MBTs experienced constant problems with their multi-fuel 700bhp Hispano-Suiza HS110 engines, which were the subject of ongoing refinement during the vehicle's service.

Although France withdrew from the NATO command structure in 1966, at the instigation of President Charles de Gaulle, France remained a member of the alliance, and committed to the defence of Europe from possible Warsaw Pact attack with its own forces stationed in the Federal Republic of Germany throughout the Cold War. A series of secret accords between US and French officials, the Lemnitzer–Ailleret Agreements, detailed how French forces would dovetail back into NATO's command structure should East–West hostilities break out.

Prior to the Six-Day War in 1967, Israel's main source of modern weapons was France, but when the French placed an embargo on the further supply of weapons following the 1967 conflict, Israel was forced to look elsewhere. One of the principal requirements was for a new main battle tank, and for a short time the Israeli Defence Forces became involved in the British Chieftain tank development programme, only to be asked to withdraw after Britain was subjected to political pressure from clients in the Arab world. With little prospect of assistance from elsewhere, the Israeli government decided that their only alternative was to launch a series of indigenous weapons production

France's AMX-30 Main Battle Tank, like the Chieftain, experienced problems with its multi-fuel engine. It nevertheless went on to be a very successful design, attracting large export orders. (Wikimedia Commons)

A French AMX-30 in action with the 6th Light Division during the Gulf War of 1991. (Via John McKenna)

Like the Chieftain, Israel's Merkava MBT featured heavily sloped armour. (IDF)

programmes, and the development of a main battle tank received high priority. The result was the Merkava (Chariot) MBT, which entered production in 1979 and was produced in several variants, each one incorporating improvements and featuring innovations. The tank was optimized for operations in the rough terrain of northern Israel and the Golan Heights and was unusual in layout, with the engine at the front and the fighting compartment to the rear. This gave enhanced frontal protection while the ammunition, kept at the back, was not only in the safest place but was also quite easily stowed in the vehicle through a rear door, making replenishment in the combat zone much safer.

The Merkava I first saw action in the Lebanon in 1982, where it performed well against Syrian T-72s. An improved version, the Merkava 2, entered service in 1973; this incorporated several improvements, including improved armour protection and fire control system. The next production version, revealed in 1989, was the Merkava Mk 3. It introduced a new suspension and transmission system and a new 120mm smooth-bore gun. A 1995 version, the Mk 3B (the Merkava Baz), has an improved fire-control system and a built-in NBC protection and air conditioning system. Also, a modular armour package was added (called 'Kasag'), making the Merkava 3 Baz Kasag one of the most protected tanks in the world.

The current generation of Mk 3 tanks is Dor-Dalet (4th generation) which includes modular add-on armour, improved tracks, an improved machine gun and integral air conditioning and NBC protection systems. The latest model is the Merkava Mk 4, which was introduced in 2004.

The design of the Merkava owed much to the British Centurion tank and its Israeli derivatives, and also to the experience gained during Israel's short-lived collaboration on the design of the Chieftain.

Adversaries

When the Chieftain was first deployed in the BAOR, its main Warsaw Pact opponent was still the T-54/55, thousands of which were in service. Elite Warsaw Pact armoured divisions, however, were in the process of rearming with the T-62 MBT, a straightforward development of the T-55. The T-62 was the first tank in the world to mount a smooth-bore main gun, a 115mm weapon that gave it much greater velocity and hitting power than the 90mm and 105mm weapons used by the western powers at that time. The T-62 entered service with the Soviet Army in 1961 and was considered by NATO to be a formidable opponent, although it was poorly armoured and had an alarming tendency to catch fire. Some 20,000 T-62s were manufactured in the Soviet Union between 1961 and 1984, and the tank was also made in Czechoslovakia and North

A straightforward development of the T-54/55, the T-62, seen here at a Soviet Armed Forces exhibition in 1972, was the first tank in the world to mount a smooth-bore main gun. (TASS)

Korea. Most of the Czech production was intended for export.

In 1966 an upgraded version of the T-62 made its appearance. This was the T-64, which served only with the Soviet Armed Forces. The first operational model, the T-64A, made its first appearance outside the USSR in 1976, when it was issued to the Guards Armoured Divisions of the Group of Soviet Forces in Germany (GSFG) in 1976, and some time later in Hungary's Southern Group of Forces (SFG). The only known variant of the T-64A was the T-64AK command vehicle, which carried additional radio equipment and a telescopic mast. The next model, the T-64B, made its appearance in East Germany and Hungary in 1981. As well as having new hull and turret armour, the T-64B was equipped to fire the Kobra (AT-8 Songster) gun-launched anti-tank missile, a radio command-guided weapon.

The T-64 was intended to complement the T-72 MBT, which entered production in 1972 and remained the principal Russian

The T-72 would have proved a formidable opponent for the Chieftain, although its fire-control and other systems were inferior to the British tank's. (TASS)

T-72s of the DDR National Volksarmee on parade in East Berlin. (Reuters)

AFV in this class until the collapse of the Soviet Union. First seen in public at a May Day parade in 1977, the T-72 was built under licence in Czechoslovakia, India, Iran, Iraq, Poland and the former Yugoslavia, where the tank was designated M-84. At least 50,000 were built and the tank is in service with 30 armies around the world. The original version of the T-72 was the T-72A, which had a laser rangefinder and improved armour, while the T-72B had additional front turret armour. The T-72BM was the first to incorporate Kontakt-5 explosive reactive armour.

Chieftain tanks wearing the special urban camouflage devised by Major Clendon Daukes of D Squadron, 4/7 Dragoon Guards, parade through West Berlin. (MoD)

Below: Former Jordanian Chieftain during the 8th Tank Day at the Military Technical Museum in Lešany.

In Service and In Action

At the peak of its deployment in Germany, the Chieftain was arguably the best Main Battle Tank in the world. Most of its defects had been eliminated during ongoing development programmes, its crews were superbly trained, and tactics had been constantly revised and improved during regular large-scale battle exercises.

Had the Chieftain been required to go to war in Europe, it would have faced the ten best armoured divisions in the Soviet Army, armed with the latest equipment, supported by ten motorized rifle divisions and assigned to the Group of Soviet Forces in Germany (GSFG). Two more tank divisions were assigned to the Northern Group in Poland, two tank and three motorized rifle divisions were with the Central Group in Czechoslovakia, and two tank and two motorized rifle divisions were with the Southern Group in Hungary. In the event of war, these groups of forces would be supported by over sixty divisions (of which 23 were armoured divisions) located in the seven military districts of European Russia closest to the NATO centre. Whereas the best Soviet divisions were Category I formations, however, many of those in the military districts were graded as Categories II or III, and would have taken some time to mobilize fully prior to deployment to the battle area.

The Chieftain-equipped divisions operated under the control of NATO's Northern Army Group (NORTHAG), which was subordinate to Allied Forces Central Europe. I British Corps, with its HQ at Bielefeld, in the 1970s comprised the 1st, 2nd, 3rd and 4th Armoured divisions, all deployed in the Hannover area, and the 5th Field Force, a brigade-sized infantry formation. In 1981–2 the Corps was reorganized, so that the 1st and 4th Armoured divisions manned the front line, with the 3rd Armoured Division in reserve. The 2nd Armoured Division was returned to the UK, where it reverted to the 2nd Infantry Division in the reinforcement role.

The other formations in NORTHAG were I West German Corps, with three armoured divisions (the 1st, 3rd and 11th) on the northern flank of I British Corps; I Netherlands Corps, with two mechanized infantry divisions and one armoured brigade, armed with Leopard tanks and based in Holland, and I Belgian Corps, with

Manoeuvring large and heavy fighting vehicles on Germany's narrow and often muddy byroads could be a dangerous occupation, as the crew of this Chieftain discovered. (MoD)

'Enemy' troops surrendering to a Chieftain during a NORTHAG exercise (MoD)

two mechanized infantry divisions, the 16th in Germany and the 4th in Belgium. The shock of any Soviet attack would therefore be initially absorbed by I West German Corps and I British Corps.

I British Corps, responsible for an area extending from a line just north of Hannover down to a line just north of Kassel, with a defensive depth of 40 miles (65km) bore a huge responsibility, for it was in this region that the Warsaw Pact forces stood a good chance of snatching a quick victory.

In all probability, the weight of any attack to fall on I British Corps would have come from the Third Soviet Shock Army, striking against the junction of I West German Corps and I British Corps. The British forces were also vulnerable to the south, where the Belgium Army relied on rapid reinforcement from Belgium to meet an attack.

The Leopard Main Battle Tanks of the West German I Corps operated on the northern flank of I British Corps. (Via H-H Schindler)

A Leopard MBT of the Royal Netherlands Army's I Netherlands Corps churns up the stubble in a West German harvest field, the harvest having been gathered in. (Via H-H Schindler)

Chieftain tanks advancing through a scene of mud and snow during Exercise Reforger, an annual exercise conducted by NATO to test the alliance's rapid reinforcement capability. (MoD)

The most exposed element of the British armoured forces during this period was the squadron of Chieftain tanks supporting the Berlin Infantry Brigade, formed in October 1953 out of the occupation force known as Area Troops Berlin. It later became part of the BAOR, being its second major component after I (BR) Corps. The three infantry battalions and armoured squadron assigned to Berlin were rotated regularly, the single armoured squadron being detached from an armoured regiment assigned to I (BR) Corps. The armoured squadron usually comprised at least eighteen Chieftain tanks.

Until 1983 the Brigade's Chieftains were camouflaged in standard green/black, but this was challenged with the deployment of D Squadron, 4/7 Dragoon Guards, whose CO, Major Clendon Daukes, realised that the vehicles did not blend in with their urban surroundings. He experimented with cardboard cut-outs of Chieftains and different types of camouflage schemes, looking for geometric patterns that would match the surrounding buildings, windows and fences. Eventually, noticing the repetition of vertical lines, he devised a rectangular pattern based on squares coloured white, grey and brown. By careful placement of different-sized squares and rectangles he was effectively able to disguise the shape of the tank, particularly from the air. The effect was similar to the blue, white and grey 'splinter' camouflage applied to warships during the Second World War.

For how long the Chieftains of the Berlin Brigade, and indeed the whole of I (BR) Corps, would have been able to hold on in the face of determined Soviet armoured attacks is questionable, but when the Chieftain's first test came, it was in an environment far removed from the plains of northwest Europe.

Iran–Iraq War

On 22 September, 1980, on the orders of President Saddam Hussein, Iraqi forces, taking advantage of the political and military chaos created by the recent Islamic revolution, invaded neighbouring Iran. The Iranians, thanks to holding actions fought by paramilitary forces and their remaining air strength, managed to slow down the Iraqi advance to the point where it became bogged down and degenerated into a war of attrition, with both armies conducting their operations in a thoroughly unco-ordinated fashion. This was particularly true of the Iranians, who lacked sufficient strength to push back and drive out the Iraqis and also had to contend with internal power struggles, one of which was led by Iran's President Banisadr. In the end, Banisadr convinced Supreme Leader Ayatollah Khomeini in Tehran (who had the final say in all state matters) to allow him to take personal command of the regular army. After Banisadr took personal command

A Leopard I of I West German Corps passing by a picturesque German village. (Via H-H Schindler)

and arrived at the front, he began planning a major offensive against the Iraqis, codenamed 'Operation Nasr' (Victory). The attack was to be carried out entirely by the regular army.

The operation began with a thrust by three armoured regiments of the 16th Qazvin Armoured Division into Khuzestan province, which was intended to relieve the city of Abadan, besieged by the Iraqi Army. The main attack was preceded by three diversionary attacks, which penetrated some five miles (eight kilometres) into Iraqi-held territory before breaking down into a series of individual engagements.

The main attack was launched on 5 January in the wake of a short but fierce artillery bombardment. It involved some 300 tanks, mostly Chieftains, organized into three brigades followed by an infantry brigade. The planning was disastrous; for a start, heavy rains had turned the terrain into a quagmire, forcing the tanks to advance slowly and in column along available roads, with their flanks exposed. Also, the advance depended on the element of surprise, which was soon swept aside when the columns were detected by air reconnaissance. Acting quickly, the Iraqis moved their 10th Armoured Brigade, equipped with Soviet T-62s, into a blocking line on the Iranian line of advance, digging their tanks into hull-down firing positions in front and on either side of the approaching enemy columns. The Iraqi armour was supported by a variety of attack helicopters, an asset which the Iranians lacked with the exception of some AH-1J SeaCobra helicopters.

The deployment of two more Iraqi armoured brigades made it possible for the Iraqis to form a three-sided box ambush, a deadly trap into which the Iranians now blundered. Contact between the opposing

The Bovington Tank Museum's Chieftain Mk 2 03 EB 83 is painted in the British Army's standard green and back camouflage scheme (Tank Museum)

forces was made on 6 January. In the first instance the Iranians attempted to batter their way through the Iraqi defences, but withdrew after taking heavy losses. They then tried to manoeuvre off-road, with the result that their tanks got stuck in the

The fighting between Iran and Iraq quickly degenerated into a form of trench warfare reminiscent of a European battleground in the First World War. (Reuters)

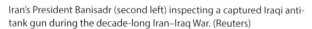

Iran's President Banisadr (second left) inspecting a captured Iraqi anti-tank gun during the decade-long Iran–Iraq War. (Reuters)

Iranian troops preparing for an attack during the Iran–Iraq War (Reuters)

mud. The first of the attacking Iranian brigades was decimated, with many of its tanks destroyed or abandoned, and the second brigade fared no better.

By the time the battle ended in an exhausted stalemate on 8 January the Iranians had lost 214 tanks, the majority of them Chieftains and at least 100 other armoured vehicles; the Iraqis had lost 45 tanks and some 50 other armoured vehicles, mostly the victims of attack helicopters. The heavy Chieftain losses,

North Korean support for Iran. This is a ZSU-23-4 radar-controlled SPAAG.

An Iranian Chieftain tank captured by the Iraqis and pressed into service. (US Army)

Aftermath: An Iraqi T-62 tank lies abandoned and derelict in Kuzhestan province, still in its hull-down position. (Wikimedia Commons)

M60A3 Pattons on Soviet built MAZ-537 transporters being removed from the battlefield after the disaster of Operation Nasr. (Reuters)

although attributable in the main to poor planning, lack of adequate training and even worse tactics, did reveal a need to strengthen the tank's frontal turret armour, which resulted in the design of the Stillbrew package.

Kuwait 1991: the Battle of the Bridges
A decade after Operation Nasr, the Chieftain was in action once more, this time with much more favourable results. At midnight local time on 2 August 1990, Iraq invaded neighbouring Kuwait. Although there had been plenty of indications that an invasion would occur, the Kuwaiti armed forces were generally not in a state of alert and the country was quickly overwhelmed, although some units managed to fight back. The spearhead of the Iraqi attack was

A view of an Iraqi T-72 main battle tank destroyed in a Coalition attack during Operation Desert Storm near the Ali Al Salem Air Base.

Kuwait's brigade of Chieftain tanks made short work of Iraq's Russian-supplied T-72s. (Via John McKenna)

units of the Republican Guard, principally the Hammurabi Mechanized Division, with two mechanized and one armoured brigades, and the Medinah Armoured Division with two armoured brigades and one mechanized. The engagements inside Kuwait mainly involved the 17th Brigade of the Hammurabi, and the 14th Brigade and 10th Armoured Brigade of the Medinah. These elite units were armed with the T-72 Main Battle Tank, Iraq's latest acquisition from the Soviet Union. Their main objective was Kuwait City.

One of the few Kuwaiti Army formations that had been placed on alert, only a couple of hours before the invasion was launched, was the 35th Armoured Brigade, which managed to field 36 of its 50 Chieftain tanks, supported by a company of

Alongside its Chieftains, the Kuwaiti Army used the M-84 MBT, a Yugoslav version of the Russian T-72. This one is ploughing through a sand berm on exercise. (Wikimedia Commons)

Liberation: the so-called Highway of Death, strewn with wrecked and abandoned Iraqi vehicles pulverized by Coalition forces during the flight from Kuwait. (via John McKenna)

The Challenger I replaced the Chieftain during the Gulf War.

Below left: A Challenger I tank during the Gulf War.

Below right: British Army M109 howitzers in action during the 1991 Gulf War. (Tank Museum)

Captured Iraqi Type 69-IIA during Operation Desert Storm.

Coalition forces advance towards Kuwait City after the expulsion of the Iraqis. (Source unknown)

The Vijayanta Main Battle Tank, seen here on display at Kannur Cantonment, was a license-built variant of the Vickers Mk 1. (Sandeep Gangadharan)

armoured personnel carriers, a company of anti-tank vehicles and an artillery battery with seven M109 155mm self-propelled howitzers. The deployment of the 35th Brigade was somewhat piecemeal but was completed by 0600, the Chieftains taking up position to the west of the interchange between Highway 70 and Sixth Ring road. Shortly afterwards, Iraqi tanks were seen approaching down the six-lane Sixth Ring Road, advancing in road columns with their flanks unsecured.

At 0645 the Chieftains of the Kuwaiti 7th Battalion began to engage the Iraqi T-72s, opening fire at a range of less than a mile and quickly halting the enemy column. The Iraqi response was slow and ineffectual. Iraqi units continued to arrive at the scene apparently unaware of the situation, allowing the Kuwaitis to engage infantry still in trucks and even to destroy a self-propelled gun that was still on its transport trailer.

At 1100 elements of the Medinah Armoured Division of the Iraqi Republican Guard approached along Highway 70 from the west. Again they were deployed in a column and actually drove past the Kuwaiti artillery and between the 7th and 8th battalions, before the Kuwaiti tanks opened fire. Taking heavy casualties, the Iraqis withdrew back to the west. After the Medinah regrouped and deployed they were able to force the Kuwaitis, who were running out of ammunition and in danger of being encircled, to withdraw south. The Kuwaitis reached the Saudi border at 1630, spending the night on the Kuwaiti side before crossing over the next morning. Their crew could take pride in the fact that their Chieftains had destroyed thirty enemy tanks for no loss to themselves.

The 35th Kuwaiti Brigade was reconstituted at Hafir al-Batin, filling its ranks with personnel who had fled their homeland, new volunteers and soldiers who had been serving abroad at the time of the invasion. Spares were purchased from the Chieftain's manufacturers and new stocks of ammunition obtained. During the

Vijayanta. India's first indigenous Main Battle Tank was built on a licensed design of Vickers MK 1 of UK origin and was introduced into service in 1965.

The Challenger I was the second tank to be fitted with Chobham armour, the other being the M1 Abrams. This tank belongs to the 1st Queen's Dragoon Guards, SFOR Operation Resolute, Bosnia, 1996. (MoD)

liberation of Kuwait in February 1991 the Chieftain-equipped brigade was designated the Shid (Martyrs) Brigade.

Chieftain Offspring

As the Chieftain progressed through its early development period, Vickers identified a requirement for a cheaper and less complex variant intended purely for export. The result was the Vickers Mk 1 Main Battle Tank, which incorporated the 105mm L7 rifled tank gun of the Centurion and the Leyland L60 engine, transmission and fire control system of the Chieftain. The tank was developed as a private venture, but when India issued a requirement for a tank very similar in concept and design, Vickers offered the MBT and it was accepted. The first two prototypes were completed in the spring of 1963 and series production began in the following year, an agreement having been reached in the meantime whereby India would also manufacture the AFV under the name Vijayanta (Victorious). Over 2,200 Vijayantas were eventually produced, and these saw combat against Pakistani forces in the war of 1971. Kuwait ordered 70 Vickers MBT Mk 1 tanks in 1968, these being delivered between 1970 and 1972. Meanwhile, Vickers continued to develop the basic Mk 1 design, installing a more powerful engine and improving the turret design to produce the Mk 3. Kenya ordered two batches of 38 Mk 3s in 1977–78, and Nigeria ordered 36 in 1981, both countries also acquired small numbers of the armoured recovery vehicle variant.

Challenger I MBT Mk 3.

A British Challenger 1 main battle tank, belonging to the Royal Scots Dragoon Guards, waits by the Basra-Kuwait Highway near Kuwait City following the retreat of Iraqi forces during Operation Desert Storm.

Challenger

It might be said that the acquisition by the British Army of the tank that would eventually replace the Chieftain, the Challenger MBT, happened by accident as the result of the cancellation of the Iranian order for its version of the Chieftain Mk 5, the Shir, following the Islamic revolution. With modifications to suit it for operations on a European battleground, the Shir design was adopted by the British Army as the Challenger I, production starting in 1983 by Royal Ordnance Leeds (taken over by Vickers Defence Systems in 1986). Production of the Challenger I continued until 1990, by which time 420 units had been built. The Challenger's hull and turret were protected by Chobham armour, developed in great secrecy in the 1960s at the British tank research centre on Chobham Common, Surrey. Composed of ceramic tiles encased within a metal framework and bonded to a backing plate and several elastic layers to give a high degree of protection against shaped charges such as high explosive anti-tank (HEAT) rounds and kinetic energy penetrators, it was first applied to the American M1 Abrams MBT, which like the Challenger saw action during the 1991 Gulf War. The Challenger I was supplanted in turn by the Challenger II, which although resembling its predecessor was in effect a new MBT.

Preservations, wrecks and relics

Fortunately for students and enthusiasts of armoured warfare, numbers of Chieftain tanks have been preserved, some in full

The Tank Museum's Chieftains demonstrate their agility during a public display. (Tank Museum)

working order, in military museums. Others, in worse condition, are to be seen scattered across military firing ranges in the United Kingdom. Heading the list of tank museums in the UK is the Tank Museum at Bovington Camp in Dorset, South West England. It is about 1 mile north of the village of Wool and 12 miles west of the port of Poole and houses an extensive collection of armoured fighting vehicles. Among the exhibits is the Chieftain G1 prototype 01 DC 87, which carried out gunnery trials at the Royal Armoured Corps Gunnery School at Lulworth, Dorset up to 1962, and the P6 Mk 1 prototype 99 SP 23. The collection also includes the Mk 2 01 EB 49 and Mk 5s 06 SP 71 and 04 EB 21, and Mk 11 03 EB 83, which is in full working order and carries out demonstrations from time to time. Finally, the museum boasts an example of the Jordanian Khalid MBT, painted in Middle East camouflage.

Also in full working order is the Norfolk Tank Museum's Chieftain Mk 2/3 02 EB 05, which was upgraded to Mk 9 standard in the course of its operational life. At one stage it was used as a special projects vehicle with RARDE, investigating various aspects of stealth technology and other classified subjects. The Norfolk Tank Museum is located at Forncett St Peter, NR16 1HZ, two miles from Long Stratton on the A140 Norwich to Ipswich road.

Another military museum in Norfolk housing a working Chieftain is the Muckleburgh Collection, sited on a former military camp at Weybourne on the north Norfolk coast. It is the largest privately owned military museum in the United Kingdom. The Chieftain is a Mk 5.

There are several Chieftain exhibits at the IWM Land Warfare Museum at Duxford, Cambridge: a Chieftain ARRV, a Chieftain Marksman Self-Propelled Anti-Aircraft Weapons System, a Chieftain Mk 6 MBT, a Chieftain Mk 10 MBT and a Churchill AVRE. Another Mk 6, 01 EB 30, is retained by the Defence College of Management and

Sound and fury: two of the Tank Museum's Chieftains carrying out a thunderous display at Bovington. (Tank Museum)

The Bovington Museums ex-Jordanian Khalid MBT. (Tank Museum)

End of the line: The sad remains of a Chieftain used as target practice on the Imber Ranges on Salisbury Plain, Wiltshire (Wikimedia Commons)

Technology at Shrivenham and bears the standard British Army green and black camouflage scheme.

The Yorkshire Air Museum at Elvington has a unique example of the Chieftain. The development of the Chieftain with a 1,000hp engine and enhanced transmission was a project by Vickers Defence Industries, in partnership with the German companies RENK, MTU and Krupp-MAK, and was intended to offer a significant performance and reliability upgrade for existing Chieftain tanks.

The first customer was to be Kuwait, whose existing Chieftains were soon to see action in the Gulf War of 1991. The MoD expressed an interest in upgrading their engineer vehicles and the BARV (Beach Armoured Recovery Vehicle) of the Royal Marines. The improved design was not developed further, however, leaving this unique prototype as the most powerful Chieftain Tank ever built.

Outside the UK, a Chieftain Mk 1 (65 MS 99) is preserved at the US Army Ordnance Museum, Aberdeen Proving Ground, Fort Benning, while Mk 2 02 EB 91 is retained at the British Army Training Unit at Suffield, Canada (BATUS) after being used as a target. A Chieftain Mk 11 is on display at the Canadian War Museum, LeBreton Flats, Canada.

A Chieftain Mk 5/5P features in Hall 5 (British and American Tanks) of the Kubinka Research Collection, Moscow. The vehicle is most probably a former Iranian Chieftain, captured by Iraq in the 1980s and donated to the former Soviet Union.

A Chieftain Mk 11 in working order is held by the Vojenske Technicke Museum at Lesany in the Czech Republic. In addition to the Chieftains listed above in established museum collections, several tanks have been purchased at Ministry of Defence auctions by private collectors and displayed individually.